Forever

Was Never

on My Mind

By Philip M. Butera

Clare + Mike
— I'm still
Thriring
over my
Annoyance
Enjoy
love
Philip

JaCol Publishing Inc.
Copyright 2023 © by JaCol Publishing Inc.
Illustrations Copyright © 2023 by JaCol Publishing Inc.
FIRST PRINTING
MONTH 2023
All rights reserved
JaCol Publishing Inc.
195 Murica Aisle
Irvine, CA 92614
818-510-2898
Editor-in-Chief: Randall Andrews
Managing Editor: Roman A. Clay
www.jacolpublishing.com

ISBN: 978-0-9890159-9-8

Cover Design—Chris Moore (Southern Printing---www.southernprintingandmarketing.net)

Cover Photo:—Denis Laperriere

Model—Nancy Clair

Table of Contents

Praise for Philip's Poetry

"I was first introduced to Philip Butera's work through 'The Apparition,' his three-act play that featured the inspiration of the Muses. With this collection, 'Forever Was Never On My Mind,' the author conjures those same muses in several playful yet poignant poems. It is a thoroughly engaging and entertaining meditation on a life of 'Walking Into Mirrors,' 'Seeing the Face of My Own Ghost,' and 'Loss, Nonetheless.' Butera's latest is highly recommended and sits on the top of my 'must-read' list."

Chris Bodor, Editor-in-Chief of Ancient City Poets, Author, Photographer, and Artist (A.C. PAPA) Literary Journal

"The sheer talent and skill of Philip Butera as a writer simply cannot be disputed. He is a language wizard when using the written word to present imagery, ideas, and feelings that are profound yet easily absorbed by the reader. Additionally, if poetry is meant to be read aloud, Butera's work is satisfying indeed."

Salvatore Alessi, Adjunct Professor of Literature, Canisius College

"Philip Butera uses words and phrases like an accomplished artist uses color and light. Excellent balance of imagery and abstraction. His command of language is broad and lush."

Nicole Washburn, Editor, Ghostwriter

"Philip Butera writes incredible poems. His vibrant language and artistic visions will have you clamoring for more."

Ann Christine Tabaka, Multi-Award-Winning Poet

"Philip Butera glides, rides, manipulates, caresses, seduces, and inhibits language. While his images and phrasing initially appear complex and constant, he manages to be clear and concise with both. To call him anything short of a verbal genius would be a denial of his unparalleled ownership of the richest of all languages."

Kathleen Bryce Niles, Editor, Comstock Review

"With raw passion and profound psychological perception, Philip's poetry pierces your innermost being."

Eva E. A. Skoe, Ph.D., Clinical Psychology, Professor of Psychology

"A significant accomplishment. It is important that people read what Philip Butera has created."

Michael Griffin, English Professor, Okanagan College Kelowna Campus

"Philip's beautifully dangerous poetry captivates the reader with intensely revealing intimacy."

Teresa Ann Frazee, Poet, Founder of the Boca Raton Museum of Art, Art and Literature Series

Acknowledgment

An editor is like an older brother who believes in tough love. Every writer needs an editor. Not a friend or neighbor whose dream was to teach third graders about grammar but who became a dental assistant. Not someone who praises your work and would hate to hurt your feelings. An editor edits. A good editor looks at every punctuation mark, every word, every sentence, and every paragraph to make sure what you are conveying is what you want to communicate.

An editor notices what you assumed and tells you unapologetically your assumption is incorrect. Their favorite phrases are "What does this mean," "Wrong word," and "Run on sentence." An editor is much like Sherlock, using a spyglass and deduction about what you have written. The editor is not critical but insightful about where the grammatical crimes have occurred. It is no time for tact. What is needed is straightforward, concise, and blunt advice.

I am lucky. My poetry editor is relentless in his guidance. He has no problem telling me what must go, what stays, and why. He distinguishes between brilliance and egotism and points it out. It's not arrogance. It is kindness. Because I know he wants my poems to be read, understood, contemplated, and appreciated.

I dedicate this book to my poetry editor Sal Alessi

Ill-Fated

I am scholarly,

detached,

uncertain,

a teardrop between

uncomfortable

and not belonging.

Like a neglected wound

I am scarred

and imply

what I don't say.

I have no illusions about distractions.

I remain

a wanderer

waiting for storms to uproot

what I find grounding.

I cannot remember a journey

without doubt

or a romance

without glossy wings–

beautiful as a rainbow

but always

ill-fated.

For

wind and time

become

errors in an abyss

refusing to concede.

As I contemplate

the unsettling darkness

of characters I've played

self-deception

curls about me.

I sought the exceptional

but found the visceral.

I have trapped words and used them as lures.

Outlined with silver garlands

they shimmered

giving me an advantage.

But I

distrusted precautions

and when

the stakes were the highest

I walked away

alone.

Bells That Toll

Did you hear the bells?

Bells that toll

must have a purpose

like love

or death.

The bells rang boldly

when I was a child.

I heard the bells

they captured my attention

like America,

like life.

I heard the bells

near a playground,

near a station,

on a back road.

Those bells sounded

and they

4

beckoned.

My mother heard the bells,

in the distance,

in the future,

she felt the motion inside her

as she wept

putting fresh flowers on my sister's grave

and my brother's.

Bells sound—

like needs,

like intentions,

like loneliness.

The bells sound.

They call.

They chime after a tragedy,

after a wedding,

after a war.

Bells,

bells

clang and bang

but

the silence

between rings

booms.

I Walked Into My Mirror Yesterday

Write down the things you want.

Read them aloud to yourself.

Dreams and imagination

are always

echoes before tragedies.

I walked into my mirror yesterday

and

I saw you–

naked with old-age freckles

on your backside.

Your legs no longer

glistening

and your hair

more silver than mine.

I continued

past the clutter found in crawl spaces

and the comments we never believed

about each other.

You heard me call

and you turned,

your breasts no longer proud,

your belly no longer flat,

and

I can no longer make up the truth.

I dislike sentimentality

but your playful smile

still dispels

the light rain

in my soul.

The angels,

who would encourage us to defy the line

between visionary and extreme long ago

now

rest on hammocks in destiny's shadow.

Their eyes are closed

realizing old photos are trials

lost in reality.

The wedding of colors

we were spilled from

are now teardrops,

and I realize neither of us will ever

gallop past

what we expect

and

paint the wind.

I See the Face of My Own Ghost

The night is no friend.

It is a heavy black overcoat

hiding away

the moonlight and stars.

Alone on a cliff,

aware of my misgivings,

I ask for clarity.

I search to

uncorrupt the darkness

but the cold sea gusts

and heavy mist

ascend from

the angry waters below

to drench me

in tears.

I fall to my knees

aware

of my fright.

In the dark nothingness

I see the face of my own ghost.

I am

an unwelcomed guest

an insignificant wisp

woven into the night's

indifference.

As If to Stifle a Cry

An arrow pierced my heart.

Not from Cupid, I'm afraid,

but from the chaos

of desires unsettled.

I recognize the bleakness of beliefs

and watch black and white become

black and blue

in scarlet flames.

Long before the upheaval

I remember the days of war

and the repetitious urge

to capture the invisible.

I hate the hatred

of one being hated.

It should be simple

as if to stifle a cry—

to find clarity with reasoning.

But as I look at the sea

devoid of boundaries

I realize

logic is futile.

A Loss, Nonetheless

I trip, I fall,

I used to be sure-footed,

now

I am sure of very little.

I turn off the news,

I turn off the noise.

I turn away from what is irrelevant,

all those loud, noisy voices out there.

What I thought was background

is now forefront—

birds chirping,

ducks gliding,

squirrels scurrying,

and

rabbits on the run.

I sit and listen

to what is anchorless;

to what is subject without a predicate.

Those sounds of life living

and not caring about the lies

we use for language.

I abandon all those worries

that I wove into myself

and that lightness

brings me to this lawn chair.

To a daily

view of simpleness.

The sweetness

of belief beyond pretense.

The life I was living,

living, what an ambiguous word,

was just

waiting for the promise

of Spring.

But I never recognized the change

when it arrived

only the silhouette

in the moonlight as it sailed away.

The ducks scold each other

yet they stay together.

A solidary Egyptian Goose

has a broken wing.

She will never fly again

every day I feed her.

She comes closer

than the others

but we never touch

and

I realize a loss can be a win

but a loss,

nonetheless.

I Wanted to Love You

I did lie to you,

but they were honest lies

my heart could not sell my soul.

When remembrances

become shadows in memory frames,

outlines blur

and what was delicate

dissolves.

I wanted to love you—

maybe I did,

perhaps I said the same to her,

and her before,

and her before.

The winds signal a warning.

Cold rain is expected

then

the gloomy

numbness of winter.

The same process

as love.

When We First Were Lovers

It never goes away—

the stardust

from those

fragile moments.

I remember

the day had not yet surrendered

its golden rays.

They shimmered

through the threadbare curtains.

We were in a yellow cottage

in a pale green bedroom

with the correct play

of fading light and sea breezes

carrying the smell of honeysuckle

from across the lake.

There was

the allure of fair naked skin

under stiff white sheets

dried by the warm winds

beneath an old

 and faded

patchwork quilt.

Delicate and young—

we seemed to fit perfectly.

No longer hiding behind our faces

and

unrestrained by concern.

Time was a kind friend,

rewarding us for every minute.

We were woven into

the impressionable peacefulness

of knowing

an equal share

was better

than a greater one.

That sweetness

of innocence

has lingered forever

when we

first were lovers.

You Are Naked Now

You are naked now.

You are special now.

I see what you don't.

I see

you will never be set free

from your perfected persona

unless you embrace

your journey into uncertainty.

Snow White and Sleeping Beauty

were characters without flesh.

You are flesh wrapped in desire

yet

denying temptation.

I am an artist

offering you

a paintbrush or a dagger

to define yourself.

Model or victim

both

can lie their weaknesses into strengths.

There are never mirrors

on wishing wells

and secrets,

and dreams

weigh heavy on thin clouds.

You can remain naked without apologizing

or

wait for the storms to come.

I Slept With Lady Macbeth

I slept with Lady Macbeth

before the witches spoke.

Her breasts were large—

milky-white kissed with pale pink.

Nude and mellifluous, our bodies met

heat and passion, exploring all desires.

How it pleased her to be touched.

Our intimacy was beyond fault,

lips everywhere without blushing.

We loved more than all the stories to be,

from time undone to moments to come.

We ran swiftly into tomorrow's distance

when an author recognized her beauty.

To chivalry, to Arthur, to Robin Hood.

Guinevere offered us a bed and Marion wept.

Soon a pen found paper and we could not remain.

Binding ourselves together, we tangled—

on damp earth and shattered glass, our obsession roared.

I slept between her soft legs, her scent intoxicating.

Finally, the moon's blueness became the bookmark.

Fate is never timely and Shakespeare had no choice.

I was erased from her thoughts,

and she became a tragic heroine

searching for reality.

I Have No Idea About Souls

I

have no idea about souls

but I feel mine

is in prison

though

there are

no bars

and

there are no words

to describe the

loneliness.

My friends are dying.

I am told we are at that age.

Eight in the last ten months

have died.

My cousin passed,

I still speak with him though.

I do our routines,

playing both roles.

Back then, we made each other laugh,

now,

I am sad.

Sad—

a word we seldom contemplate.

Oh, we say it, we bandy *sad* about,

but we rarely understand the seriousness of the word.

Maybe because it has only three letters

and it is easy to say.

Sad—

much more manageable

than despondent

and we never use the word mournful.

That's a word found in stylish mysteries.

Here is another word—

disheartened.

A word used when all the other words

have wept themselves to sleep

and this one—disheartened—

is available.

My friends and my cousin are dead,

and I feel

hollow.

Just another word

for sad.

That Night

That night—

the gods held up a gigantic sheet of black silk,

and I was caught between the darkness and the fabric.

Frightened, I asked, "What is night?"

A huge bird with fiery red eyes

and iridescent indigo wings

carried me to a rushing stream

where plots hatched,

and conversations ended in voids.

That night,

cold-dark nothing,

nothing

in its horrid nakedness descended.

The burden of loneliness

filled the tiny damp space where I had hidden.

I heard the sky's scaffold

Collapsing

and memories of distances traveled filled my mind.

That night—

the huge bird,

now blind and dying,

asked, "When is night?"

I held her close,

and she listened to the beat of my heart.

Darkness seeped into blackness

and

between dreams

I fell asleep.

Many Demons Live Inside My Head

Not one, not two, but many demons live inside my head.

They constantly bicker while gambling to sway my behavior.

They laugh while slicing through my thoughts.

There are the good-bad demons, the bad-bad demons, pure evil demons, and the mentally unfit to-be-in-my-head monsters.

There is no leader— they are a gang of vanishing questioners always on the periphery, constantly motioning, continually demanding, and always directing.

They all have one voice that they stole from me.

I was a child, dancing in the warm rain.

I was dreaming of what it would be like when the sun scoots the clouds away and the expanse would be blue, becoming even bluer.

I would be clothed in happiness, living in the softness of light and promises.

But dogs howl—it's their nature, and my father continued to drink.

While I write, some demons are giddy, others scamper into a pack and encircle all the redemptive phrases, while the most frightening hover over my sanity and curse the clarity in the distance.

A famous artist said, "There is something terribly cruel about reality."

Is that why the demons have gathered in my head?

They slither through the chaotic vernacular of my unconscious, exploiting expression from experience and diminishing pleasure.

Once, in tears, I asked a demon why they chose me.

Every voice heard it, and they became silent.

There was that loud silence you feel in dreams.

My mind echoed what I had asked.

I waited and waited then a horrific cold shiver

went through me.

They Are Balloons

They are balloons, colorful and complete.

Gauzy clouds in the late afternoon blue sky

are their background

and a peeking sun with a golden welcoming.

I am a distant figure changing with perspective

continually failing to catch up with me

even when the stars say I have.

The white strings from the balloons

are wrapped around her wrist

and it is obvious she is comfortable

with herself wearing loose reds and oranges

dismissing the contrast.

She has no shadow

only a late summer wide-eyed enthusiasm.

She smiles

but not at me.

She smiles

because the wind is refreshing and the day is lovely

and because she has balloons

for no reason,

she just has them

and they complement her mood.

I have a small knife in my pocket

and not much faith in myself.

She is happy and I hate her for not being ambiguous,

because I am confined within me

while she glides,

glides with her balloons tied to her wrist.

For me—there is no up or down,

only a rattling of obstruction

and a clattering of confusion.

I like things sharp with no memory.

She is genuine and filled with delight

animated and alive

like her balloons.

Beyond sheer happiness in a realm

where multiple balloons

would rather be tied to her wrist

than travel heavenward.

She has shoulder-length light brown hair

and round sunglasses,

singing an old song, I almost recollect.

Her voice is familiar,

I think.

Or is it the voice in my head I am hearing?

I get closer to her.

I open my knife in my pocket

confessing my insecurities

while I watch the girl

with balloons tied to her wrist.

The cheerful girl knows she is exceptional,

sitting on the soft grass untangling the balloons.

One by one, she sets them free.

One by one, the wind gently sweeps them up

and as one white balloon

becomes trapped in a large tree's thick branches

I wrap my fist

around the knife's blade

and squeeze.

I Am Kind Enough to Lie

Like a flash of reality

or insanity

I can be charming

or condescending.

Yes,

I can become

a caricature of myself.

A rush of rhetoric

from a mouth

that bleeds contempt.

I can scintillate your imagination

with a wreath of twinkling stars

raining delicate rose petals

praising

the landscape of your soul.

I was born

on a cold January evening

while a storm raged

and that icy winter chill

has never left me.

Picasso died in his bed drawing.

I will be falling from a

cliff too high

and landing in a round bed

between Circe and Calypso.

I know I said,

"You are different,"

but I am kind enough to lie

because I find it pleases you.

I speak tenderly,

for sweet venom

is best served as pleasingly

as permission to remain.

Now,

before thought

becomes a tango with rules

uncross your legs

for I am

the first in line

to devour you.

The Exit

Eyes wide,

fear of closing them again.

My heart is racing.

It's 3:00 AM

and I am chasing my breath—

another nocturnal anxiety attack.

Doom grabs hold,

stunned.

I am

unable to scream,

unable to move.

The tentacles of fright

overcome

my certainty.

Panic slithers

to the forefront of my thoughts.

I temper fear

with logic, but question

if I am thinking

rationally.

Experiencing conflicting feelings

with all explanations

limited to a gasp.

My mind jeers

the next sleep

will be without escape,

without waking.

Pacing

from room to room,

the internal storm

continues to rage

and

without sentiment

my thoughts begin to yield.

Is this an exit

or the exit?

I Heard All the Gods Cackling

I turned to follow,

I sensed a presence

to guide me.

I wrapped myself

around my feelings

though

I knew they were misleading.

All my thoughts

were exhaled

and shards from mirrors

surrounded me.

I was cold,

I was tired,

I hated myself

for trying to find

what

I could never comprehend.

There was no light

only a feeling of lightness.

I walked until the darkness went black.

I was where destiny

greeted weariness,

where self-pity

and self-loathing

became venomous partners,

vying to take lives.

I heard all the Gods cackling.

I followed

what I knew to be true of myself.

How insignificant

it seemed.

It was nothing.

Nothing!

Nothing in its vastness,

Nothing in its complexity,

Nothing in its emptiness.

And Hope,

Hope

was a momentary silhouette on fine dust.

I looked,

I prayed,

I no longer had an alibi for being.

So, the outcome was swift.

A roar from the gods-

worthless!

I knew there were no gods

Only me,

Only me

and I was powerless

to

help myself.

It Is a Time When Dreams Are Allegorical

There is the glow of the setting sun as a briny wind mingles with the smell of fried food and sugary treats.

The amusement park is alive with frenzied movement and framed by glittering lights.

Girls with cotton candy wear Bikini tops and high-waisted sailor shorts, while young men sport striped Breton shirts and tight black slacks.

You and I eat funnel cake and laugh, barely aware of Sugar Mountain's silhouette in the distance.

It is a time when dreams are allegorical, filled with a flurry of inventiveness without interpretations or need for regret.

With my hands in your back pockets we wait in line to twirl and whirl in a shiny silver rocket.

With my thoughts in your mind, we wait impatiently for darkness when we can dash past the noisy roller coaster to a cottage bedroom out of sight to be naked and alone.

It Is Neither a Hippopotamus Nor an Elephant

It is neither a

hippopotamus

nor an elephant

charging

across

this dark room.

But a cold insistence,

nothing identifiable

that tears can dispel.

It is a missingness

of ever feeling whole.

An insistence

that saturates

the

hollowness.

Waves

a thousand feet tall

47

crest and pummel

scattering what is always becoming

but never fulfilled.

It is bitterly

unexplainable

to understand

what

is louder

then it sounds.

The dark room

darkens further.

I pull the shades in my mind

and coalesce

without tampering.

I sting myself

with thoughts

too harsh

to remember

and

slip off a cliff

to be trampled

by

passing gazelles.

Under a Dying Rainbow of Words

It doesn't last,

as soon as things become promising

I destroy

the chances of it succeeding.

I extract what would make a difference

and leave what is left to languish

and wither.

Reason

can't overcome fear.

Fear,

the color that changes time

and

can never be explained.

When I see myself

it is always in the past,

like a painter walking through his wet painting

but never getting a drop on himself.

I feel fraudulent

and I have a need

to apologize to my reflection.

Unfortunately, we can't know a time

before we are born

where the sharp hooks of life are sketches

being drawn.

As I back away

from understanding

the hazy atmosphere of unknowing

isolates me.

I appreciate more

why there must be a purgatory

a whirlwind of cleansing

before salvation.

Or is that

just

self-acceptance?

I have neither begun nor ended.

I am what evaporates in the night

while hiding from the dark.

I work my way out of every dream

and I find shelter

in the bitter tyranny

of illusions.

I have a sickness that screams

without a voice.

I am alone

under a dying rainbow of words

trapped by my existence

on a birthstone ship of terrors

with thoughts

that will never

set sail.

As the Aperture Opens Wide

No baggage and no contrition.

Unsure,

am I careless or careful?

The mesh of a fishnet boundary

slyly maneuvered.

Tattered edges,

an invitation for bad intentions.

Aware

I am pandering to danger,

like Hermes chasing Melinoe,

I find the distraction

of shimmering images

and

light through

champagne

more fascinating

than embellished dreams.

I welcome the tussle

as the swell matures

and my chin

parts the sweet flesh

of smooth legs.

The hourglass reminds us

that causes and cures are clouds in motion.

I am no fool,

I realize pity has its laws.

Yet, there is a spurring curiosity

for contradictions.

An appetite

to hear tolling bells

while pleasure beckons.

I love

the lingering scent of perfume

on inner thighs,

as eyes

with disapproving approval

question a thirst never quenched.

There is a tiny white stitch

deep within the silky black barrier.

A twilight

never to be reached.

Thoughts gather,

for temptation is but a blindfold

over a threshold

moist with deceptions.

While Hera sees Aphrodite in her mirror

I follow the white line,

a pantomime villain disguised as a seducer.

The visual changes

but the intention remains.

Nakedness opens a world of metaphors

and

with a cruel delight

the obvious becomes addictive.

But redemption

is a dark shadow on a forgotten gravestone.

Never

charming lines of poetry

applauding dreamy stars.

In a world devoid of frankness,

promotional gestures

bring meaning to nonsense.

I regale the fragrance

of an ageless mystery.

Legs become opened scissors

and I giggle to myself

as the aperture

opens wide.

You Once Called Me Mad

My world,

my outlook,

my emotions

experience all seasons at once

and I am

always prepared.

I waited for your call,

a call to the wild.

You once called me mad

and I agreed

but my acting

created the person

I have become

and

I am an actor.

You loved my kisses—

your legs spread easily

but you

disliked

my perfected indifference.

Words and meanings

became confused

and our obsession subsided.

Passion

diluted to apathy

and desire

withered.

The jagged edges

of resentment

took hold.

The curtain came down.

Now, you have found someone to follow you

and I am

rehearsing

lines

for a new play.

A Raven Among Crows

He drove a candy apple red Oldsmobile ninety-eight,

and I waved to him

from the picture window as he left for work.

He was always leaving for work,

being at work, or going to work.

I wondered what work was.

I never wanted to go there,

to work,

because it made my mother sad

and me lonely.

Across from my small white house with a green awning

was a playground.

I spent my youth there.

We were kids with Italian last names,

but we were all Phil Rizzuto hitting home runs

in the summer

and Rocky Marciano

winning by a knockout in the fall.

During the long cold winter there were snowmen,

snow angels, snowball fights,

and fantasies

of spring.

I overheard words like leads, bids, and deals.

They all meant the same.

My mother and I would spend

the weekends catching buses to my grandmother's.

If we stayed home

my mother would sit at the end

of the white couch with the gold trim

her eyes dashing between the television and the

picture window,

while I played with tiny rubber cowboys

and

plastic blocks

on the green rug with green swirls.

I learned that work came with after work

at taverns and bars.

Time

was an ocean of waves

that capsized dreams

and

held

hope hostage.

The seasons changed and the playground disappeared.

My father was a raven among crows.

He drove a Cadillac

and we had a summer home

on the lake.

But the distance between my parents

never mended.

Restless,

I roamed,

wanting to fill the emptiness,

to understand the unspoken vocabulary

inside me.

Sometimes

I was a shoe with a broken heel.

On a few occasions

I excelled

and wore a smile.

I learned daydreams

gave you the answers

you want,

rarely the truth.

I found friendship and warmth,

even love.

I circled,

nested at times

but I never took flight

among the

blackbirds.

There Are Dollops of Fresh Air

I am a different species,

old,

yet alive

I live in a basket

of guidelines

of tunes to play

and skins

to wear.

There are

dollops

of fresh air

between

reminisces about songs

with love in the lyrics

and knowing

idealism

degrades with age.

These days my dreams

get out of bed before me

and

my words

create old photos

that pour like thick honey.

With time, weariness

and vulnerability takes hold.

I have a need

to say something,

and once it is said,

there is no need for it to be said again

but

I don't know when it should be said.

I follow the shrieks of old habits,

reading,

learning,

and thinking.

At times,

when the day has untwisted itself

I try to rouse

the essence of my soul.

I imagine a bridge,

I reach for a butterfly

made of the most beautiful words.

I slip.

I fall.

The

water welcomes me

but offers no sympathy—

no sympathy

at all.

The Countless Thorns

My story is imprisoned in a dream.

She came forward

interrupting the night.

My slumbering imagination,

a brush stroke.

She was surrounded

by fine lines of light.

I embellished the scene.

She was a swirl of colors

so rich

I was overwhelmed by the sight of her.

We were about to kiss

then time

through sleep,

swept me away.

As I yelled,

"Why?"

67

stars drew closer.

Unaware

I was awake

I darted across the sky.

Falling through the dream

into thick rose bushes.

I wildly

reached for her

but

the countless thorns

dug

into my eyes

and I remained

alone.

The Cheek Kiss

The phone rings.

It is her.

She asks, "Do you have company?"

I say, "No."

The car lights flash in the windows.

The dogs bark.

She is at the door.

I say, "Hi."

The cheek kiss.

Awkward moments.

"White wine?" I ask.

"Rum and coke."

I say, "Sure."

My heartbeats

Are louder than my voice.

"How are you?" she asks.

I say, "Fine."

How does it happen?

Two people who tangled in bed for years,

loved intimately,

kissed passionately,

touched feverishly,

spoke sincerely

now sit across from each other

hoping for wanted forgiveness.

Big brown eyes, long legs,

and a dress a bit too short, she enters my purgatory.

She whirls my emotions and the sting reminds me

that I still love her.

I want it to be then—years ago,

with Christmas cheer

and joy punctuated with smiles after every word.

But I know her rehearsed movements,

her impatience with things not in her control.

"You look thinner."

I say, "Really?"

She sighs, "Why aren't you out?"

I look deep into her.

Deeper than eyes can penetrate.

Passion is the cruelest emotion.

It's the animal whose jaw never releases its prey.

"Why are you here?" I ask.

"I have met someone younger than us.

He's my beautiful indulgence

like you were many years ago when we met.

But I can't let you go.

Once, you said you would die for me.

I need that.

Would you commit suicide?"

The clutter of the past means recognizing the familiar.

I turn up the music, sweet jazz, listenable jazz,

jazz, she never quite grasped.

She was a country girl,

quick to memorize lyrics

and expects you to be grateful.

Her perfume lingers

though she has left.

Which is more uncomfortable,

the silence under the music, the loneliness,

or the request?

My thoughts pace,

too frightened to be definitive.

Forgive and forget

must separate

and

only one word can resound.

I travel from one dream to another.

They become tourists

asking permission to leave.

The phone rings.

It is her.

She asks if I have company.

I say, "No."

The car lights flash in the windows.

The dogs bark

She is at the door

I say, "Welcome."

The cheek kiss.

Awkward moments.

"Rum and coke?" I ask.

She says, "A double."

"How are you?" I ask.

"Good. How are you?" She asks politely.

I pick up one of the dogs, the dachshund.

He presses his head to my chest

as if listening to my heartbeat.

"I'm dying," I say with a snicker.

She collects the white and brown Shih Tzu

and places him in the chair she has just vacated.

Her movements are calm and deliberate.

She selects a framed photo of us

taken when the sun shone

even in winter.

She opens a drawer

placing it under an older photo of us.

Her car's rear lights flash in the windows.

I take her untouched drink and bring it to my lips

recalling,

"Every truth starts with a fantasy."

Between a Windmill and a Lighthouse

I didn't expect to forget myself

but just in case

I kept a small mirror in my

pocket.

It was round,

I found it in my mother's

jewelry drawer.

On the reverse was

the profile of a woman from long ago

when bombs were dropping

and rife

was a word the newspapers used often.

She wore a fashionable hat

and a fur collar scarf

around her neck.

One graceful hand held the case

while the other powdered her cheek.

The tin cover was charcoal and cream,

and it never left the drawer.

I never saw my mother put it in her purse.

I had the feeling

it was a toss-away gift

from my father,

something neither purchased nor sought

just something he found

probably in a Tavern

and later

given to my mother.

I looked for my face in the mirror

but I

saw my parents

disliking each other.

With a protective smugness

I listened

as you accused me

of having few of the virtues

you found attractive.

You walked out the door

with obligatory sobs

and hurt expression

through the garage

to your new convertible.

You had already packed your bags

so there was no need to slow down.

You passed through and out,

a lover

I neglected to know.

I sat on the leather couch

leaning forward over the glass coffee table

with the scattered art books.

Remorse and nostalgia

began their remake of tattered rainbows.

Before me, The Italian Renaissance, The Surrealists,

and French Impressionists.

All these years,

were they there to help or deceive?

I read once that art is atmosphere encountering light,

and I wonder

if desires

are just a careless combination of clashing colors.

I have no idea if my soul is resentful

of the life I have lived.

When I needed clarity

hopeful narratives and emotional sincerity

wore boxing gloves.

I was between a windmill and a lighthouse

frightened

I was the cause of my parents

unhappiness.

The heartbeat of the ocean is a wave

and that wave

is indifferent to how it encounters the shoreline.

You are gone

and I am turning pages.

You can't sweeten sorrow,

and an apology is just a symptom

of emotional hunger.

A Turbulent Blur

I will remain broken

untied to commonplace stories

or gestures

of enabling conditions

for happiness.

At times, I am a violent seascape

self-assured and reckless

at other times

I am unraveling, frightened

of my reflection.

In my dreams, I am impatient,

lawless

but never the victim.

Victims are emotional,

I am

self-contained,

both director and actor,

a forger of documents

stating

my purpose.

I see the face of my past.

I experiment

with knowledge and crisis

and loathe

relationships

that require

exuberant detail and splendor

leaving no permission

to bewilder.

There are moments to explore

and moments to linger

and times

when the intention

is only entanglement.

No subject

or presumption

just diffused light

through

a glass of champagne.

What if love is an extraction?

An ironic affection

sucking

at the breast

of penance.

I remember that first time

we undressed each other.

You left scars on my back

and asterisks on my beliefs.

I have learned since,

illumination

always

questions passion.

Occasionally,

I have been fortunate

but more often

I have been

what can never be tethered—

a turbulent blur.

I Am a Man of Wintriness

There are cold thoughts

caked in ice

etched without warning.

Final good-byes forever melt

never to dissipate.

They remain an icicle

no matter how warm

the reverie.

I look into a mirror.

It cracks;

the image wants to disappear

but it

becomes many reflections

compelled

by

shadows.

When obscurity is the aim

time is different.

One tomorrow

follows the other

suspended between

anger and resentment

creating

endless sorrow.

I am a man of wintriness

affected by relentless storms.

My accountability

is to darkness

then chaos.

My reality is textured

with chilly ambiguity.

A soul is but

a sheath of relentless mistakes

craving forgiveness.

Life remains strange

yet familiar,

a tumbling of

deceit and nostalgia.

Like brambles

hidden after a snowfall

I spill from doubt,

an eclipse

spent from tragedy.

I remain detached,

aloof

and warmth

is only antagonized

by the wintriness

that is me.

I See a Metaphor

I have become indifferent

to things that are too unfriendly to be true.

The curling of day

into select misfortunes.

The mention of places

too high to reach.

I overhear conversations,

the needs of why

and I detach from myself

knowing once ignited,

fear permeates

all illusions of trust.

At dusk's arrival,

I see a metaphor.

With the world to roam,

an innocent doe is trapped in

a barbed wire fence.

Consciousness blurs

and

I see my reflection

kissing the breast

of a lover

dead

from the mind down.

Ideas

Ideas

wrapped with thorns

swirl

inside my mind.

A dangerous serpent basks

in my thoughts.

It is kept alive

by the slow process of letting go.

Madness—

the most heartless kind

is regret trapped in stained glass

without

any means of escape.

You can neither sugarcoat guilt

nor soothe pain.

You must change and grow

or

chase fading

perfumes of the day.

Love Dies

The **Fall**

begins

with the realization of the

elevation

you are falling from.

The **Fall**

is

continual

but you encounter

what

you believe

is a

lifeline.

Unfortunately

it is not anchored,

and

looking down,

the height

is higher

than

you expected.

The **Fall**

seems like

a breath in a bad dream

but

your eyes are open

and

the descent

is not

an illusion.

The **Fall**

accelerates.

Deception creeps into

your thoughts

and you think

you will be

saved.

That is a rare

and you

have

never been

lucky.

Your lover

pushed you

to see

if you could fly.

Your fears have been

confirmed

you are not

whom you appear

to be.

As you

experience

the **Fall,**

you break.

Love dies.

Can Anyone See the Distance

It was all at the water's edge.

When the Angel slipped

and I caught her.

She asked, "You are broken?"

My tears moistened her wings,

and when we kissed there was a rainbow

tethered to my heart.

Held captive by the storm within,

not deserving but unfortunate,

I asked, "Can anyone see the distance?"

She smiled, "A question philosophers defer to sages

when poets give flight to words."

At midnight all the stars became a beloved melody.

The Angel's figure was faultless,

yet she was elusive.

We tangled in dreams and imaginings

knowing intimacy is an unrelenting motion

held captive.

On my knees, I pulled her body to me

The pain was immediate

and I fell

into her damnation of endless images,

of everything unreachably real.

In the womb of night,

the Angel confused me with all things presumptive.

I became a faint reflection of a fading impression.

Like a drop of water about to fall,

one thought remained,

how unforgiving is lovelessness?

Teetering between then and now,

I desperately reached for the Angel,

her smile remained,

but she

had disappeared.

I See Vastness and You See Confinement

While

slivers of sunlight

slice through moody gray clouds

you casually ask, "If I love you."

Feeling the numbness of hypocrisy

I pick up my palette

and choose ultra-marine and crimson.

With my brush,

I replace you with an ocean creature.

Not a mermaid, not a siren

but

something real,

traveling out to sea

becoming one

with the unknowable thoughts

at the fringe of my mind.

However,

it is me and not you

that is cast adrift

some distance between relevance and reality.

The ocean understands indecision

it is always contemplating.

Waves come near, then disappear.

"Do I love you?"

You need answers.

I want interpretations.

Our hearts beat

binding us in time

but expectations have dissipated.

I see vastness

and

you see confinement.

We are ripples

meandering away

as the ocean continues

to ebb and flow.

Quietly Gone

I should be dead.

Quietly gone.

The deep depression would be set free.

Where does it go when it leaves?

Maybe like a hurricane, it just devours itself.

Should I start to name the depression cycles

I experience?

Should I give myself warnings

that soon my mask will dissolve?

That my reflection will not be the cartoon character

I loathe.

To those who care,

keep your distance—

please don't come near.

I pretend

and I lie.

Depression

is a wounded animal trapped in an

opened cage.

I hate the pretense of being normal when I am not.

I hate the practice of caring when I do not.

I hate, hating

though

adoring

would never be me.

No more pills every morning.

No more chemicals displacing what my mind originates.

No more dulled-down and sifted-out feelings.

If I were quietly gone,

the trap of being trapped would vanish.

The strain on reason would snap.

The polite excuses would disappear.

Through the thickness of smothered thoughts,

a tiny voice screeches,

madmen frighten everyone,

Should I be dead?

Your Violet Lips Parted

"Remember, there will be numerous ways to die,"
Athena said before she created the garden.

Behind a weeping willow in full bloom
you undressed and held your breasts to me.
I kissed each nipple
and my hand slipped between your legs.
You were moist
yet cool,
and a shiver of darkness
ran through me.

The soft cooing of the mourning dove
was a signal for you to begin.
On a picnic table
smelling of fresh flowers and warm moments
you asked me to recline.
You selected the sharpest knife.

Without guilt or blame,

you carefully sliced open my chest

to watch my heartbeat.

Moments passed,

the garden became a theatre

for us to perform.

Your expression changed from amusement to inquiring

and your bright eyes widened.

You suggested,

"Why don't we exchange hearts?"

Your violet lips parted

as you handed me a scalpel.

The blade was precise,

I found that vanishing point,

whoosh,

gradations of scarlet colors

spilled

into everything false

about ourselves.

The soft cooing became

loud screeching

and

the wind carried a chill.

The sun was setting

and

we couldn't find our way.

"Seagulls weave a path," said Athena.

But birds cannot mend

what

is not meant to be.

It has been years.

Your heart has stopped

and

I am unoccupied.

How lonely

it is

to be wrong.

The Sleepy Nightness

Mirrors change time

and anxiety crawls into memories

becoming

a prison of deception and regret.

I remain on your side of the bed,

I can smell

the sleepy nightness

that clung to you.

You left weeks ago

yet

you permeate the room.

You said, "I am going, and nothing you say can convince
me to stay."

My mind intends to follow,

to mend all the broken pieces

and leave what is left

behind.

How Interesting

I am told

not all people dislike themselves.

I find that interesting

because

I cannot understand

how

some wouldn't.

BIO

Philip M. Butera grew up in Buffalo, NY, earned a B.S. degree From Gannon College in Erie, PA, served in the U.S. Navy then received an M.A. in Psychology from Simon Fraser University in Vancouver, Canada. He lives in Boynton Beach, Florida. He is on Facebook. Visit his website: www.philipbutera.com Email – philip@philipbutera .com

Books by

Philip M. Butera

Poetry:

Mirror Images and Shards of Glass

Dark Images at Sea

I Never Finished Loving You

Falls From Grace, Favor and High Places

Novels:

Caught Between

Caught Between is also a PodCast Radio Series
https://wprnpublicradio.com/caught-between-teaser

Art and Mystery: The Missing Poe Manuscript

Far From Here (Winter 2024)

Play:

The Apparition